Proceedings
general officers 1
His Excelle
Washington

commander in chief of the Army of the United States
of America respecting Major John André, adjutant
general of the British Army

John André

Alpha Editions

This edition published in 2024

ISBN 9789362516749

Design and Setting By
Alpha Editions
www.alphaedis.com
Email - info@alphaedis.com

EXTRACTS OF LETTERS

From General Washington, *to the* President *of* Congress.

Robinson's House, in the Highlands, Sept. 26, 1780.

SIR,

I have the honor to inform Congress, that I arrived here yesterday about twelve o'clock, on my return from Hartford. Some hours previous to my arrival Major General Arnold went from his quarters, which were this place, and, as it was supposed, over the river to the garrison at West Point, whither I proceeded myself, in order to visit the post. I found General Arnold had not been there during the day, and on my return to his quarters he was still absent. In the mean time, a packet had arrived from Lieut. Colonel Jameson, announcing the capture of a John Anderson, who was endeavouring to go to New York with several interesting and important papers, all in the hand writing of General Arnold. This was also accompanied with a letter from the prisoner, avowing himself to be Major John Andre, Adjutant General to the British army, relating the manner of his capture, and endeavouring to shew that he did not come under the description of a spy. From these several circumstances, and information that the General seemed to be thrown into some degree of agitation, on receiving a letter a little time before he went from his quarters, I was led to conclude immediately that he had heard of Major Andre's captivity, and that he would, if possible, escape to the enemy, and accordingly took such measures as appeared the most probable to apprehend him. But he had embarked in a barge and proceeded down the river, under a flag, to the Vulture ship of war, which lay at some miles below Stoney and Verplank's Points. He wrote me a letter after he got on board. Major Andre is not arrived yet, but I hope he is secure, and that he will be here to-day. I have been and am taking precautions, which I trust will prove effectual to prevent the important consequences which this conduct, on the part of General Arnold, was intended to produce. I do not know the party that took Major Andre, but it is said that it consisted only of a few militia, who acted in such a manner upon the occasion, as does them the highest honor, and proves them to be men of great virtue. As soon as I know their names, I shall take pleasure in transmitting them to Congress.

Paramus, October 7, 1780.

SIR,

I have the honour to enclose Congress a copy of the proceedings of a Board of General Officers in the case of Major Andre Adjutant General to the British army. This officer was executed in pursuance of the opinion of the Board, on Monday, the 2d instant, at 12 o'clock, at our late camp at Tappan. Besides the proceedings I transmit copies of sundry letters respecting the matter, which are all that passed on the subject, not included in the proceedings.

I have now the pleasure to communicate the names of the three persons who captured Major Andre, and who refused to release him, notwithstanding the most earnest importunities and assurances of a liberal reward on his part. Their names are, *John Paulding, David Williams, and Isaac Van Wert.*

GEORGE THE THIRD.

PROCEEDINGS

OF A Board of General Officers,

Held by Order of his Excellency General Washington, commander in chief of the army of the United States of America, respecting Major Andre, Adjutant General of the British army, September the 29th, 1780, at Tappan, in the State of New York.

PRESENT,

Major General Greene, President, Major General Lord Stirling, Major General St. Clair, Major General The Marquis de la Fayette, Major General Howe, Major General The Baron de Steuben, Brigadier General Parsons, Brigadier General Clinton, Brigadier General Knox, Brigadier General Glover, Brigadier General Patterson, Brigadier General Hand, Brigadier General Huntington, Brigadier General Starke, John Lawrence, Judge-Advocate General.

Major Andre, Adjutant General to the British army was brought before the Board, and the following letter from General Washington, to the Board, dated Head Quarters, Tappan, September 29th, 1780, was laid before them and read.

Gentlemen,

Major Andre, Adjutant General to the British army, will be brought before you for your examination. He came within our lines in the night, on an interview with Major General Arnold, and in an assumed character; and was taken within our lines, in a disguised habit, with a pass under a feigned name, and with the inclosed papers concealed upon him. After a careful examination, you will be pleased, as speedily as possible, to report a precise state of his case, together with your opinion of the light in which he ought to be considered, and the punishment that ought to be inflicted. The Judge Advocate will attend to assist in the examination, who has sundry other papers relative to this matter, which he will lay before the Board.

I have the honour to be, Gentlemen, Your most obedient and humble servant, G. WASHINGTON.

The Board of General Officers convened at Tappan.

The names of the officers composing the Board were read to Major Andre, and on his being asked whether he confessed the matters contained in the letter from his Excellency General Washington to the Board, or denied them, he said, in addition to his letter to General Washington, dated Salem, the 24th September, 1780, (which was read to the board, and acknowledged by Major Andre, to have been written by him,) which letter is as follows:

Salem, 24th Sept. 1780.

SIR,

What I have as yet said concerning myself, was in the justifiable attempt to be extricated; I am too little accustomed to duplicity to have succeeded.

I beg your Excellency will be persuaded, that no alteration in the temper of my mind, or apprehension for my safety, induces me to take the step of addressing you, but that it is to secure myself from an imputation of having assumed a mean character for treacherous purposes or self interest. A conduct incompatible with the principles that actuated me, as well as with my condition in life.

It is to vindicate my fame that I speak and not to solicit security.

The person in your possession is Major John Andre, Adjutant General to the British army.

The influence of one commander in the army of his adversary is an advantage taken in war. A correspondence for this purpose I held, as confidential (in the present instance) with his Excellency Sir Henry Clinton.

To favour it, I agreed to meet upon ground not within posts of either army, a person who was to give me intelligence; I came up in the Vulture man of war for this effect, and was fetched by a boat from the shore to the beach. Being there I was told that the approach of day would prevent my return, and that I must be concealed until the next night. I was in my regimentals and had fairly risked my person.

Against my stipulation, my intention and without my knowledge before hand, I was conducted within one of your posts. Your Excellency may conceive my sensation on this occasion and will imagine how much more I must have been affected, by a refusal to reconduct me back the next night as I had been brought. Thus become a prisoner I had to concert my escape. I quitted my uniform *and was passed another way in the night without the American posts to neutral ground, and informed I was beyond all armed parties and left to press for New York. I was taken at Tarry Town by some volunteers.*

Thus as I have had the honor to relate was I betrayed (being Adjutant General of the British army) into the vile condition of an enemy in disguise within your posts.

Having avowed myself a British officer I have nothing to reveal but what relates to myself, which is true on the honour of an officer and a gentleman.

The request I have to make your Excellency, and I am conscious I address myself well, is, that in any rigour policy may dictate, a decency of conduct towards me may mark, that though unfortunate I am branded with nothing dishonourable, as no motive could be mine but the service of my king, and as I was involuntarily an impostor.

Another request is, that I may be permitted to write an open letter to Sir Henry Clinton and another to a friend for cloaths and linen.

I take the liberty to mention the condition of some gentlemen at Charles-Town, who being either on parole or under protection, were engaged in a conspiracy against us. Though their situation is not similar, they are objects who may be set in exchange for me, or are persons whom the treatment I receive might affect.

It is no less. Sir, in a confidence in the generosity of your mind, than on account of your superior station that I have chosen to importune you with this letter.

I have the honour to be, with great respect, Sir, Your Excellency's most obedient and most humble servant, JOHN ANDRE, Adjutant General.

His Excellency General Washington. &c., &c., &c.

That he came on shore from the Vulture sloop of war in *the night* of the twenty-first of September instant, somewhere under the Haverstraw mountain; that the boat he came on shore in carried *no flag,* and that he had on a surtout coat over his regimentals, and that he wore his surtout coat when he was taken; that he met General Arnold on the shore, and had an interview with him there. He also said, that when he left the Vulture sloop of war, it was understood he was to return that night; but it was then doubted, and if he could not return he was promised to be concealed on shore in a place of safety, until the next night, when he was to return in the same manner he came on shore; and when the next day came he was solicitous to get back, and made enquiries in the course of the day, how he should return, when he was informed he could not return that way and he must take the route he did afterwards. He also said, that the first notice he had of his being within any *of our posts,* was, being challenged by the sentry, which was the first night he was on shore. He also said, that the evening of the twenty-second of September instant, he passed *King's Ferry between our posts of Stoney and Verplank's Points,* in the *dress he is at present in, and which he said was not his regimentals,* and which dress he procured, after he landed from the Vulture and when he was within our posts, and that he was proceeding to New York, but was taken on his way at Tarry Town, as he has mentioned in his letter, on Saturday the twenty-third of September instant, about nine o'clock in the morning.

The following papers were laid before the Board and shewn to Major Andre, who confessed to the board that they were found on him when he was taken, and said they were concealed in his boot, except the pass:

A pass from General Arnold to John Anderson, which name Major Andre acknowledged he assumed.

Artillery orders, September 5, 1780.

Estimate of the force at West Point and its dependencies, September 1780.

Estimate of men to man the works at West Point, &c.

Return of ordnance at West Point, September 1780.

Remarks on works at West Point.

Copy of a state of matters laid before a council of war, by his Excellency General Washington, held the 6th of September 1780.

JOHN BALDWIN

WASHINGTON'S HEAD QUARTERS AT TAPPAN

THE BRAVE VOLUNTEER

GEN. LORD STIRLING.

Stirling

MAJ. GEN. HENRY KNOX

Knox

A letter signed *John Anderson*, dated Sept. 7, 1780, to Colonel Sheldon, [FN-1] was also laid before the Board, and shewn to Major Andre, which he acknowledged to have been written by him, and is as follows:

New York, the 7th Sept. 1780.

SIR,

I am told my name is made known to you, and that I may hope your indulgence in permitting me to meet a friend near your out posts. I will endeavour to obtain permission to go out with *a flag* which will be sent to Dobb's Ferry on Monday next, the 11th, at twelve o'clock, when I shall be happy to meet Mr. G____. [FN-2] Should I not be allowed to go, the officer who is to command the escort, between whom and myself no distinction need be made, can speak on the affair.

Let me entreat you. Sir, to favour a matter so interesting to the parties concerned, and which is of so private a nature that the public on neither side can be injured by it.

I shall be happy on my part in doing any act of kindness to you in a family or property concern of a similar nature.

I trust I shall not be detained, but should any old grudge be a cause for it, I shall rather risk that, than neglect the business in question, or assume a mysterious character to carry on an innocent affair, and, as friends have advised, get to your lines by stealth.

I am, Sir, with all regard, Your most obedient humble servant, John Anderson.

Col. Sheldon.

[FN-1] Less it should be supposed that Colonel Sheldon, to whom the above letter is addressed, was privy to the plot carrying on by General Arnold, it is to be observed, that the letter was found among Arnold's papers, and had been transmitted by Colonel Sheldon, who, it appears from a letter of the 9th of September to Arnold, which inclosed it, had never heard of John Anderson before. Arnold in his answer on the 10th, acknowledged he had not communicated it to him, though he had informed him that he expected a person would come from New York, for the purpose of bringing him intelligence.

[FN-2] It appears by the same letter that Arnold had written to Mr. Anderson, under the signature of Gustavus. His words are "I was obliged to write with great caution to him, my letter was signed Gustavus to prevent any discovery in case it fell into the hands of the enemy."

Major Andre observed that this letter could be of no force in the case in question, as it was written in New York, when he was under the orders of General Clinton, but that it tended to prove that it was not his intention to come within our lines.

The Board having interrogated Major Andre about his conception of his coming on shore under the sanction of a flag, *he said, That it was impossible for him to suppose he came on shore under that fashion;* and added, that if he came on shore under that sanction, he certainly might have returned under it.

Major Andre having acknowledged the preceding facts, and being asked whether he had any thing to say respecting them, answered, He left them to operate with the Board.

The examination of Major Andre being concluded, he was remanded into custody.

The following letters were laid before the Board, and read:—Benedict Arnold's letter to General Washington, dated September 25, 1780, Col. Robinson's letter to General Washington, dated September 25, 1780, and General Clinton's letter, dated the 26th September, 1780, (inclosing a letter of the same date from Benedict Arnold) to General Washington.

On board the Vulture, Sept. 25, 1780.

SIR,

The heart which is conscious of its own rectitude, cannot attempt to palliate a step which the world may censure as wrong; I have ever acted from a principle of love to my country, since the commencement of the present unhappy contest between Great Britain and the Colonies; the same principle of love to my country actuates my present conduct, however it may appear inconsistent to the world, who very seldom judge right of any man's actions.

I have no favour to ask for myself. I have too often experienced the ingratitude of my country to attempt it; but from the known humanity of your Excellence, I am induced to ask your protection for Mrs. Arnold, from every insult and injury that the mistaken vengeance of my country may expose her to. It ought to fall only on me; she is as good and as innocent as an angel, and is incapable of doing wrong. I beg she may be permitted to return to her friends in Philadelphia, or to come to me as she may choose; from your Excellency I have no fears on her account, but she may suffer from the mistaken fury of the country.

I have to request that the inclosed letter may be delivered to Mrs. Arnold, and she permitted to write to me.

I have also to ask that my cloaths and baggage, which are of little consequence, may be sent to me, if required their value shall be paid in money.

I have the honour to be, with great regard and esteem, Your Excellency's most obedient humble servant, B. ARNOLD.

His Excellency General Washington.

N. B. In justice to the gentlemen of my family, Col. Varrick and Major Franks, I think myself in honour bound to declare, that they, as well as Joshua Smith, Esq; (who I know is suspected) are totally ignorant of any transactions of mine, that they had reason to believe were injurious to the public.

Vulture, off Sinsinck, Sept. 25, 1780.

SIR,

I am this moment informed that Major Andre, Adjutant General of his Majesty's army in America, is detained as a prisoner, by the army under your command. It is therefore incumbent on me to inform you of the manner of his falling into your hands; He went up with a flag at the request of General Arnold, on public business with him, and had his permit to return by land to New York; Under these circumstances Major Andre cannot be detained by you, without the greatest violation of flags, and contrary to the custom and usage of all nations; and as I imagine you will see this matter in the same point of view as I do, I must desire you will order him to be set at liberty and allowed to return immediately; Every step Major Andre took was by the advice and direction of General Arnold, even that of taking a feigned name, and of course not liable to censure for it.

I am, Sir, not forgetting our former acquaintance, Your very humble servant, BEV. ROBINSON, Col. Loyl. Americ.

His Excellency General Washington.

New York, Sept. 26, 1780.

SIR,

Being informed that the King's Adjutant General in America has been stopt, under Major General Arnold's passports, and is detained a prisoner in your Excellency's army, I have the honour to inform you, Sir, that I permitted Major Andre to go to Major General Arnold, at the particular request of that general officer. You will perceive, Sir, by the inclosed paper, that a flag of truce was sent to receive Major Andre, and passports granted for his return, I therefore can have no doubt but your Excellency will immediately direct, that this officer has permission to return to my orders at New York.

I have the honour to be, your Excellency's most obedient and most humble servt. H. CLINTON.

His Excellency General Washington.

New York, Sept. 26, 1780.

SIR,

In answer to your Excellency's message, respecting your Adjutant General, Major Andre, and desiring my idea of the reasons why he is detained, being under my passports, I have the honour to inform you, Sir, that I apprehend a few hours must return Major Andre to your Excellency's orders, as that officer is assuredly under the protection of a flag of truce sent by me to him for the purpose of a conversation which I requested to hold with him relating to myself, and which I wished to communicate through that officer to your Excellency.

I commanded at the time at West Point, had an undoubted right to send my flag of truce for Major Andre, who came to me under that protection, and having held my conversation with him, I delivered him confidential papers in my own hand writing, to deliver to your Excellency, thinking it much properer he should return by land, I directed him to make use of the feigned name of John Anderson, under which he had by my direction to come on shore, and gave him my passports to go to the White Plains on his way to New York. This officer cannot therefore fail of being immediately sent to New York, as he was invited to a conversation with me, for which I sent him a flag of truce, and finally gave him passports for his safe return to your Excellency; all which I had then a right to do, being in the actual service of America, under the orders of General Washington, and commanding general at West Point and its dependencies.

I have the honour to be, your Excellency's most obedient and very humble servant, B. ARNOLD.

His Excellency Sir Henry Clinton.

LE BARON STEUBEN

Le Baron de Steuben

GEN SIR WILLIAM HOWE

The Board having considered the letter from his Excellency General
Washington respecting Major Andre, Adjutant General to the British army,
the confession of Major Andre, and the papers produced to them,

REPORT to His Excellency, the Commander in Chief, the following facts, which appear to them relative to Major Andre.

First, that he came on shore from the Vulture sloop of war in the *night* of the twenty-first of September instant, on an interview with General Arnold, *in a private and secret manner.*

Secondly, that *he changed his dress within our lines, and under a feigned name, and in a disguised habit,* passed our *works at Stoney and Verplank's Points,* the evening of the twenty-second of September instant, and was taken the morning of the twenty-third of September instant, *at Tarry Town, in a disguised habit,* being then on his way to New York, *and when taken,* he had in his possession several papers, which contained *intelligence for the enemy.*

The Board having maturely considered these facts, DO ALSO REPORT to His Excellency General Washington, that Major Andre, Adjutant General to the British army, ought to be considered as a Spy from the enemy, and that agreeable to the law and usage of nations, it is their opinion, he ought to suffer death.

Nath. Greene, *M. Genl.,* President. *Stirling, M. G. Ar. St. Clair, M. G. La Fayette, M. G. R. Howe, M. G. Stuben, M. G. Saml. H. Parsons, B. Genl. James Clinton, B. Genl. H. Knox, Brig. Genl. Artillery. Jno. Glover, B. Genl. John Patterson, B. Genl. Edwd. Hand, B. Genl. J. Huntington, B. Genl. John Starke, B. Genl.* John Lawrence, *J. A. Genl.*

APPENDIX.

Copy of a Letter from Major Andre, Adjutant General, to Sir Henry Clinton, K. B. &c. &c.

Tappan, Sept. 29, 1780.

SIR,

Your Excellency is doubtless already apprised of the manner in which I was taken, and possibly of the serious light in which my conduct is considered, and the rigorous determination that is impending.

Under these circumstances, I have obtained General Washington's permission to send you this letter; the object of which is, to remove from your breast any suspicion, that I could imagine I was bound by your

Excellency's orders to expose myself to what has happened. The events of coming within an enemy's posts, and of changing my dress, which led me to my present situation, were contrary to my own intentions, as they were to your orders; and the circuitous route, which I took to return, was imposed (perhaps unavoidably) without alternative upon me.

I am perfectly tranquil in mind, and prepared for any fate, to which an honest zeal for my King's service may have devoted me.

In addressing myself to your Excellency on this occasion, the force of all my obligations to you, and of the attachment and gratitude I bear you, recurs to me. With all the warmth of my heart, I give you thanks for your Excellency's profuse kindness to me; and I send you the most earnest wishes for your welfare, which a faithful, affectionate, and respectful attendant can frame.

I have a mother and three sisters, to whom the value of my commission would be an object, as the loss of Grenada has much affected their income. It is needless to be more explicit on this subject; I am persuaded of your Excellency's goodness.

I receive the greatest attention from his Excellency General Washington, and from every person, under whose charge I happen to be placed.

I have the honour to be, With the most respectful attachment, Your Excellency's most obedient and most humble servant, JOHN ANDRE, *Adjutant General.*

(Addressed) *His Excellency General Sir Henry Clinton, K. B. &c. &c. &c.*

Copy of a letter from His Excellency General Washington, to His Excellency Sir Henry Clinton.

Head Quarters, Sept. 30, 1780.

SIR,

In answer to your Excellency's letter of the 26th instant, which I had the honour to receive, I am to inform you, that Major Andre was taken under such circumstances as would have justified the most summary proceedings against him. I determined, however, to refer his case to the examination and decision of a Board of General Officers, who have reported, on his free and voluntary confession and letters,—"That he came on shore from the Vulture sloop of war in the night of the twenty-first of September instant," &c. &c. as in the report of the Board of General Officers.

From these proceedings it is evident Major Andre was employed in the execution of measures very foreign to the objects of flags of truce, and such as they were never meant to authorise or countenance in the most distant degree; and this gentleman confessed, with the greatest candor, in the course of his examination, "That it was impossible for him to suppose he came on shore, under the sanction of a flag."

I have the honour to be your Excellency's Most obedient and most humble servant, G. WASHINGTON.

(Addressed) *His Excellency Sir Henry Clinton.*

In this letter. Major Andre's of the 29th of September to Sir Henry Clinton, was transmitted.

New York, 29, Sept. 1780.

SIR,

Persuaded that you are inclined rather to promote than prevent the civilities and acts of humanity, which the rules of war permit between civilized nations, I find no difficulty in representing to you, that several letters and messages sent from hence have been disregarded, are unanswered, and the flags of truce that carried them, detained. As I ever have treated all flags of truce with civility and respect, I have a right to hope, that you will order my complaint to be immediately redressed. Major Andre, who visited an officer commanding in a district at his own desire, and acted in every circumstance agreeable to his direction, I find is detained a prisoner; my friendship for him leads me to fear he may suffer some inconvenience for want of necessaries; I wish to be allowed to send him a few, and shall take it as a favour if you will be pleased to permit his servant to deliver them. In Sir Henry Clinton's absence it becomes a part of my duty to make this representation and request.

I am. Sir, your Excellency's Most obedient humble servant, JAMES ROBERTSON, *Lt. General.*

His Excellency General Washington.

Tappan, Sept. 30, 1780.

SIR,

I have just received your letter of the 29th. Any delay which may have attended your flags has proceeded from accident, and the peculiar circumstances of the occasion,—not from intentional neglect or violation. The letter that admitted of an answer, has received one as early as it could be given with propriety, transmitted by a flag this morning. As to messages, I am uninformed of any that have been sent.

The necessaries for Major Andre will be delivered to him, agreeable to your request.

I am, Sir, Your most obedient humble servant, G. WASHINGTON.

His Excellency Lieut. General Robertson, New York.

GEN. THE MARQUIS DE LAFAYETTE.

New-York, Sept. 30. 1780.

SIR,

From your Excellency's letter of this date, I am persuaded the Board of General Officers, to whom you referred the case of Major Andre, can't have been rightly informed of all the circumstances on which a judgment ought to be formed. I think it of the highest moment to humanity, that your Excellency should be perfectly apprized of the state of this matter, before you proceed to put that judgment in execution.

For this reason, I shall send His Excellency Lieut. General Robertson, and two other gentlemen, to give you a true state of facts, and to declare to you my sentiments and resolutions. They will set out to-morrow as early as the wind and tide will permit, and wait near Dobbs's ferry for your permission and safe conduct, to meet your Excellency, or such persons as you may appoint, to converse with them on this subject.

I have the honour to be, your Excellency's Most obedient and most humble servant, H. CLINTON.

P. S. The Hon. Andrew Elliot, Esq., Lieut. Governor, and the Hon. William Smith, Chief Justice of this province, will attend His Excellency Lieut. General Robertson.

H. C.

His Excellency General Washington.

Lieut. General Robertson, Mr. Elliot, and Mr. Smith came up in a flag vessel to Dobb's ferry, agreeable to the above letter. The two last were not suffered to land. General Robertson was permitted to come on shore, and was met by Major General Greene, who verbally reported that General Robertson mentioned to him in substance what is contained in his letter of the 2d of October to General Washington.

New York, Oct. 1, 1780.

SIR,

I take this opportunity to inform your Excellency, that I consider myself no longer acting under the commission of Congress; Their last to me being among my papers at West Point, you Sir, will make such use of it, as you think proper.

At the same time, I beg leave to assure your Excellency, that my attachment to the true interest of my country is invariable, and that I am actuated by the same principle which has ever been the governing rule of my conduct, in this unhappy contest.

I have the honour to be, very respectfully, Your Excellency's most obedient humble servant, B. ARNOLD.

His Excellency General Washington.

Greyhound Schooner, Flag of Truce,
Dobbs's Ferry, October 2, 1780.

SIR,

A note I have from General Greene, leaves me in doubt if his memory had served him, to relate to you with exactness the substance of the conversation that had passed between him and myself, on the subject of Major Andre. In an affair of so much consequence to my friend, to the two armies, and humanity, I would leave no possibility of a misunderstanding, and therefore take the liberty to put in writing the substance of what I said to General Greene.

I offered to prove, by the evidence of Colonel Robinson and the officers of the Vulture, that Major Andre went on shore at General Arnold's desire, in a boat sent for him with a flag of truce; that he not only came ashore with the knowledge and under the protection of the General who commanded in the district, but that he took no step while on shore but by direction of General Arnold, as will appear by the inclosed letter from him to your Excellency.

Under these circumstances I could not, and hoped you would not, consider Major Andre as a spy, for any improper phrase in his letter to you.

The facts he relates correspond with the evidence I offer; but he admits a conclusion that does not follow. The change of cloaths and name was ordered by General Arnold, under whose direction he necessarily was, while within his command. As General Greene and I did not agree in opinion, I wished, that disinterested gentlemen of knowledge of the law of war and nations, might be asked their opinion on the subject; and mentioned Monsieur Knyphaufen, and General Rochambault.

I related that a Captain Robinson had been delivered to Sir Henry Clinton as a spy, and undoubtedly was such; but that it being signified to him that you were desirous that this man should be exchanged, he had ordered him to be exchanged.

I wished that an intercourse of such civilities, as the rules of war admit of, might take off many of its horrors. I admitted that Major Andre had a great share of Sir Henry Clinton's esteem, and that he would be infinitely obliged by his liberation; and that if he was permitted to return with me, I would engage to have any person you would be pleased to name set at liberty.

I added, that Sir Henry Clinton had never put to death any person for a breach of the rules of war, though he had, and now has, many in his power. Under the present circumstances, much good may arise from humanity, much ill from the want of it. If that could give any weight, I beg leave to add, that your favourable treatment of Major Andre, will be a favour I should ever be intent to return to any you hold dear.

My memory does not retain with the exactness I could wish, the words of the letter which General Greene shewed me from Major Andre to your Excellency. For Sir Henry Clinton's satisfaction, I beg you will order a copy of it to be sent to me at New York.

I have the honour to be, your Excellency's Most obedient and most humble servant,
JAMES ROBERTSON.

His Excellency General Washington.

New York, October 1, 1780.

SIR,

The polite attention shewn by your Excellency and the Gentlemen of your family to Mrs. Arnold, when in distress, demand my grateful acknowledgment and thanks, which I beg leave to present.

From your Excellency's letter to Sir Henry Clinton, I find a Board of General Officers have given it as their opinion, that Major Andre comes under the description of a spy; My good opinion of the candor and justice of those Gentlemen leads me to believe, that if they had been made fully acquainted with every circumstance respecting Major Andre, that they would by no means have considered him in the light of a spy, or even of a prisoner. In justice to him, I think it my duty to declare, that he came from on board the Vulture at my particular request, by a flag sent on purpose for him by Joshua Smith, Esq. who had permission to go to Dobbs's ferry to carry letters, and for other purposes not mentioned, and to return. This was done as a blind to the spy boats; Mr. Smith at the same time had my private directions to go on board the Vulture, and bring on shore Col. Robinson, or Mr. John Anderson, which was the name I had requested Major Andre to assume; At the same time I desired Mr. Smith to inform him, that he should have my protection, and a safe passport to return in the same boat, as soon as our business was compleated. As several accidents intervened to prevent his being sent on board, I gave him my passport to return by land. Major Andre came on shore in his uniform (without disguise) which with much reluctance, at my particular and pressing instance, he exchanged for another coat. I furnished him with a horse and saddle, and pointed out the route by which he was to return. And as commanding officer in the department, I had an undoubted right to transact all these matters; which, if wrong, Major Andre ought by no means to suffer for them.

But if, after this just and candid representation of Major Andre's case, the Board of General Officers adhere to their former opinion, I shall suppose it dictated by passion and resentment; and if that Gentleman should suffer the severity of their sentence, I shall think myself bound by every tie of duty and honour, to retaliate on such unhappy persons of your army, as may fall within my power, that the respect due to flags, and to the law of nations, may be better understood and observed.

I have further to observe, that forty of the principal inhabitants of South Carolina have justly forfeited their lives, which have hitherto been spared by the clemency of His Excellency Sir Henry Clinton, who cannot in justice extend his mercy to them any longer, if Major Andre suffers; which in all probability will open a scene of blood at which humanity will revolt.

Suffer me to intreat your Excellency, for your own and the honour of humanity, and the love you have of justice, that you suffer not an unjust sentence to touch the life of Major Andre.

But if this warning should be disregarded, and he suffer, I call heaven and earth to witness, that your Excellency will be justly answerable for the torrent of blood that may be spilt in consequence.

I have the honour to be, with due respect, your Excellency's Most obedient and very humble servant, B. ARNOLD.

His Excellency General Washington.

WASHINGTON, LAFAYETTE & GREENE

BRIG GEN GLOVER

MAJ. GEN. JOHN STARK

John Stark

Tappan, Oct. 1, 1780.

SIR,

Bouy'd above the terror of death, by the consciousness of a life devoted to honourable pursuits, and stained with no action that can give me remorse, I trust that the request I make to your Excellency at this serious period, and which is to soften my last moments, will not be rejected.

Sympathy towards a soldier will surely induce your Excellency and a military tribunal to adopt the mode of my death to the feelings of a man of honour.

Let me hope, Sir, that if ought in my character impresses you with esteem towards me, if ought in my misfortunes marks me as the victim of policy and not of resentment, I shall experience the operation of these feelings in your breast, by being informed that I am not to die on a gibbet.

I have the honour to be, your Excellency's Most obedient and most humble servant, JOHN ANDRE, *Adj. Gen. to the British army.*

The time which elapsed between the capture of Major Andre, which was on the morning of the 23d of Sept. and his execution, which did not take place till 12 o'clock on the 3d of October;—the mode of trying him;—his letter to Sir Henry Clinton, K. B. on the 29th of September, in which he said, "I receive the greatest attention from his Excellency General Washington, and from every person under whose charge I happen to be placed;"—not to mention many other acknowledgments which he made of the good treatment he received;—must evince, that the proceedings against him were not guided by passion or resentment. The practice and usage of war were against his request, and made the indulgence he solicited, circumstanced as he was, inadmissible.

Milton Keynes UK
Ingram Content Group UK Ltd.
UKHW030627061024
449204UK00004B/245

9 789362 516749